D0569490

DISCARDED

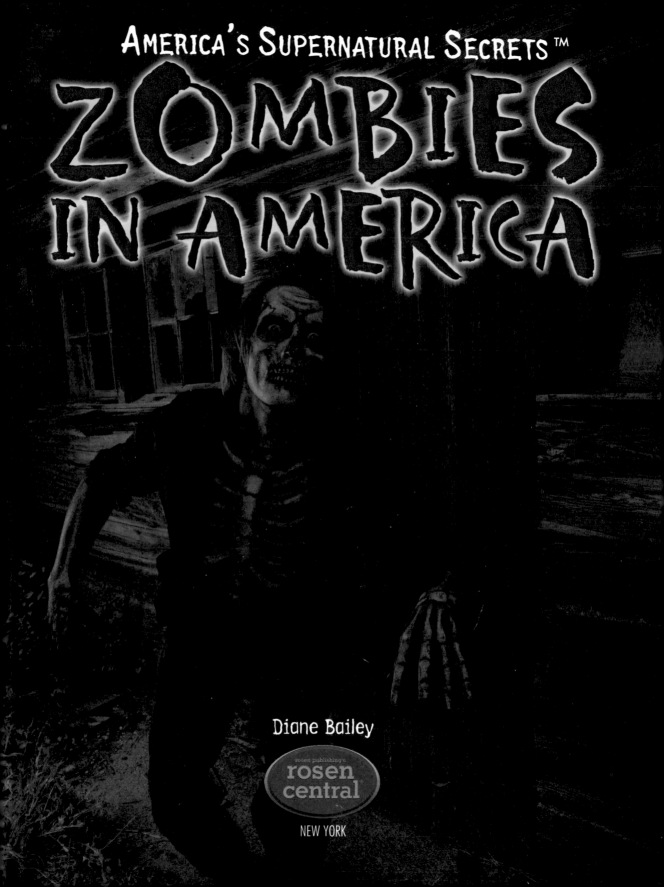

AMERICA'S SUPERNATURAL SECRETS™

ZOMBIES IN AMERICA

Diane Bailey

rosen publishing's
rosen
central

NEW YORK

Published in 2012 by The Rosen Publishing Group, Inc.
29 East 21st Street, New York, NY 10010

Library of Congress Cataloging-in-Publication Data

Bailey, Diane, 1966–
Zombies in America/Diane Bailey. — 1st ed.
    p. cm. — (America's supernatural secrets)
Includes bibliographical references and index.
ISBN 978-1-4488-5529-2 (library binding)—
ISBN 978-1-4488-5576-6 (pbk.)—
ISBN 978-1-4488-5577-3 (6-pack)
1. Zombies—United States. I. Title.
GR581.B35 2012
398'.45—dc23

2011018012

Manufactured in the United States of America

CPSIA Compliance Information: Batch #W12YA: For further information, contact Rosen Publishing, New York, New York, at 1-800-237-9932.

Contents

Introduction

Zombies are hardly ever attractive. They tend to have parts of their bodies falling off. They're covered in blood, and their clothes are ripped. Maybe worst of all, they smell bad. It wouldn't be a stretch, when a zombie shows up for breakfast, to say, "You look like death." Because, in fact, zombies are dead. They just happen to be walking around.

Most people are familiar with this image of a zombie. In movies, zombies are usually portrayed as ugly and stupid. They are also dangerous, not because they have any great powers, but because they have one purpose: to eat living humans. And even though they're often slow and clumsy, they are also very determined. After all, they don't have anywhere else they need to be—unless you count the grave!

A zombie is a reanimated corpse—in other words, a dead person who can act like he's still alive. He can move around like a living person, even though he's dead. You are not very likely to encounter a "movie zombie" as you're walking down the street. You're not very likely to encounter a real zombie, either, but some people believe that zombies really exist.

Voodoo is a religion that began in Africa. It then moved throughout the world as African people were brought to other countries as slaves. It is especially common in the country Haiti. From there, it moved into the United States. Followers believe that powerful voodoo masters called bokors can create zombies and turn them into their own personal slaves. Some evidence suggests there is a scientific basis for zombiism. However, instead of magic, the bokors use drugs on their victims.

Most people believe that is not possible to actually turn the dead into the undead. But that does not mean there are not zombies among us.

A horde of people dressed up as bloodied zombies descend upon the Lincoln Memorial in Washington, D.C., during the Worldwide Zombie Invasion in 2010.

Chapter 1

Zombies in New Orleans

In the 1700s and 1800s, New Orleans, Louisiana, was a central point for the slave trade in the United States. As slaves from Africa and the West Indies were brought into the country, they brought their belief in voodoo with them. Voodoo is a combination of an African religion, vodun, and Catholicism.

Many black people in New Orleans practiced voodoo. Powerful voodoo kings and queens would cast their spells and sell their gris-gris, which are charms to ward off evil spirits. They might also summon voodoo's primary god, which was represented by a snake known as Li Grand Zombi. Voodoo kings and queens were among the most feared people in New Orleans. In some legends, they faced off against each other. It made for a powerful battle—especially when they brought their zombies.

The Zombie War

One spring day in 1838, a woman named Black Cat Mama Couteaux came out of the Louisiana swamps and into the city of New Orleans. She did not come alone. Instead, she brought an army with her—an army of zombies. Mama Couteaux had decided she wanted to control the voodoo business in New Orleans, and she was ready to fight to do it.

Good luck charms such as these are used extensively in voodoo, a religion that has its roots in Africa and later became a common religion in Central America and parts of the United States.

Mama Couteaux must have been a frightening figure. In the stories told about her, she wore a belt and a necklace that had more than a thousand dried and shriveled tongues hanging off them. She was a powerful bokor. To make and control her zombies, she bit out the tongues of the dead people and kept them.

Leading her zombies into battle, Mama Couteaux first went to Congo Square, a place where black people gathered to hold ceremonies. There, she confronted the city's other voodoo masters, who had sent their own zombies. It's said that this battle lasted for more than a month. Some of Mama Couteaux's zombies were killed. But the other side suffered even greater casualties. As the war progressed, however, the other New Orleans voodoo kings and queens finally gained the upper hand and defeated her.

Bottled Up

Recycling is a good idea, but not if zombie bottles clutter up your counter. You might want to think twice before you toss them in the bin. In West African tradition, people believed spirits could be trapped inside bottles. They would put colored bottles on trees in their yards. One popular color was bright blue, a traditional color of voodoo. Evil spirits would be attracted to the pretty bottles and enter them. Once inside, the spirits became the property of the bottle's owner and came under his or her complete control.

Colored glass bottles are put on branches to create a "bottle tree." In West African tradition, people can trap evil spirits in the bottles to ensure they can do no harm.

Maybe Mama Couteaux's luck ran out, or her spells stopped working. Or maybe, as some say, she just got distracted. During the war, her husband, Rudolph, reportedly was killed after he lost a bet and got into a fight. Mama Couteaux was devastated. She did not want to live without him, so she did what she did best: she brought him back as a zombie!

After she lost the war, Mama Couteaux took her husband, and the remains of her zombie army, and fled west to Marshall, Texas. Perhaps the competition wasn't as great there as it was in New Orleans because she was able to establish a successful voodoo practice. She sold spells that would bring love and others that would bring money. But Mama Couteaux had a mean streak as well. It was said she could—and did—turn entire families into zombies if they dared to cross her. Sometimes she demanded money from people in return for not zombifying them.

Mama Couteaux eventually died, and when she did, people say that zombies around the country, created by her, simply fell on the spot, since she no longer controlled them. But a few remained. Mama Couteaux had grown rich in her lifetime, and according to legend, her fortune is buried on the grounds of her estate in Texas, where fifty of her zombies still stand guard.

Dr. John

In the early 1800s, the reigning king of New Orleans voodoo was a man named John Montenet, also called Dr. John. The stories of his personal history report that he was a prince from the African country of Senegal. He was sold into slavery, but later his master freed him. He traveled the world before coming to New Orleans. There, he established himself as a free black man and even owned slaves himself.

Dr. John began practicing voodoo. His home in New Orleans was filled with the paraphernalia he needed to ply his trade. There were human skulls, embalmed scorpions, and stuffed lizards. All sorts of mysterious powders and potions were scattered about. Some of his spells and charms were routine voodoo work, such as mixing love potions and herbal remedies, and providing protection to children. He also conducted séances and told fortunes.

In the eighteenth and nineteenth centuries, some black people in Louisiana gathered in places like Congo Square to conduct voodoo ceremonies, events that often frightened many white people.

But there was a darker side as well. As a busy voodoo king, Dr. John was in need of some assistants. Rather than hire them, he created them—in the form of zombies. These undead underlings did more than just boring household tasks. Dr. John also assigned them the "dirty work." He needed a steady supply of body parts for his voodoo spells, so when night fell, he sent his zombies to raid the dark graveyards of New Orleans for buried corpses.

It's also said that Dr. John trained other voodoo masters. One of his favorites was a young girl whom he called Little Sister Sally. He taught her the rituals

Take a Seat

Dr. John is known as being one of the most powerful bokors of all time. But where did he learn his dark arts? Legend says that, on moonless nights, he would sit on a throne in St. Louis Cemetery Number One in New Orleans. There, he would talk to the Devil, who taught him more than a hundred ways to turn someone into a zombie. It's also said that the Devil turned Dr. John himself into a zombie. However, Dr. John got a better deal than most. For his special student, the Devil made him a living, immortal zombie.

of voodoo and shared with her his spellbook, which contained a hundred different ways to create a zombie. But Little Sister Sally would be more than just Dr. John's student. When she turned seventeen, Dr. John turned her into a zombie and took her as his bride.

Marie Laveau and Li Grand Zombi

Even today, more than a hundred years after she died, the best known of all the New Orleans voodoo queens is still Marie Laveau. There was actually more than one Marie Laveau, but the first one was the most famous. She practiced in the first half of the nineteenth century. Laveau was a powerful woman in antebellum New Orleans. People came to her for help and healing. One time, she was able to help free a man from prison. Other times, she comforted those who were doomed to death.

Citizens both black and white respected, and often feared, her powers. Part of Laveau's business was finding out information about people that could be used against them. She was able to influence people just by suggesting that she might be able to cause them harm or that she could protect them from harm.

MARIE LAVEAU.

Marie Laveau, the voodoo queen, was both feared and revered by the citizens of New Orleans in the nineteenth century. In this drawing, she is shown in the final years of her life.

Some believe that she was trained by Dr. John himself and could raise the dead. People would whisper about the wild voodoo rituals she held, where blood was spilled and she danced with a snake called Li Grand Zombi.

In the voodoo religion, the zombie might have been a mindless servant, but Li Grand Zombi was something else altogether. This was one of the religion's great gods, represented by a serpent. Scholars believe the word "zombie" comes from the African word *nbzambi*, which means "god." It can also refer to a person's spirit, or soul. A bokor, by controlling a person's soul, created a zombie.

Was Marie Laveau able to create zombies? Even if she could, did she? No doubt few people would have wanted to risk angering the powerful voodoo queen. However, they were probably safe either way. Historical records show that Laveau was devoted to healing and other good uses of her powers.

Chapter 2

Out of Haiti

Some people scoff at the idea of zombies being real. But in Haiti, they do not laugh. There, many people insist that zombies exist, and they may be right. These are not zombies who have been resurrected from death. Instead, evidence suggests that a living person can be drugged and turned into someone who behaves like a zombie.

The fear of being made into a zombie is so great that the Haitian government even passed a law making it a crime. The law said, "It shall also be qualified as attempted murder the employment which may be made against any person of substances which, without causing actual death, produce a lethargic coma more or less prolonged. If, after the administering of such substances, the person has been buried, the act shall be considered murder no matter what result follows."

Perhaps this law discouraged some bokors, but the Haitian people would say that it did not stop them all.

In the Fields

One evening in the 1920s, American author William Seabrook listened as his Haitian friend, Constant Polynice, told him a story of zombies. Polynice assured Seabrook that zombies were not just a superstition—they were very real.

In Haiti, men dressed as zombies conduct a ceremonial ritual. Voodoo, and its recognition of zombies, is an integral part of the Haitian culture.

Seabrook wrote a book about his experiences in Haiti called *The Magic Island*. In it, he remembered Polynice saying, "At this very moment, in the moonlight, there are zombies working on this island, less than two hours' ride from [here]....I will show you dead men working in the cane fields."

Polynice then went on to tell a story of how, in 1918, many workers were needed to help in Haiti's sugarcane fields. One headman, named Ti Joseph, showed up with a group of people and registered them for jobs. The workers did not talk, but Ti Joseph said it was because they were not used to the noise and were frightened. He asked that they be assigned to a remote area. The reason for this, however, was not actually because of noise. It was because his workers were not even people—they were zombies. Ti Joseph did not want them to be recognized by someone who had known them in life. For a while, he was able to command the zombies to collect their pay for himself. He and his wife were careful to guard them closely. One thing they could not let the zombies do was eat salt or meat. That would make their consciousness return.

One day, Ti Joseph's wife took the zombies to a celebration in town. There, she allowed them to have a sweet treat, thinking it would be safe. However, the food contained salt and the zombies returned to life. Immediately they began walking back to their homes. When they arrived, Seabrook wrote, "The people of their village…recognized among them fathers, brothers, wives, and daughters whom they had buried months before." The zombies, however, did not recognize their loved ones. Instead, they made straight for the graves from which they had been taken.

After Polynice told this story, he took Seabrook to see zombies who were toiling in the fields. The author was struck by the dead look in their eyes. He wrote, "[The face] was vacant, as if there was nothing behind it. It seemed not only expressionless, but incapable of expression."

Felicia Felix-Mentor

An African American author named Zora Neale Hurston also traveled to Haiti, where she heard stories of zombies and even believed that she encountered one herself. In her book *Tell My Horse*, she wrote, "I had the rare opportunity to see and touch an authentic case. I listened to the broken noises in its throat…I know that there are zombies in Haiti. People have been called back from the dead."

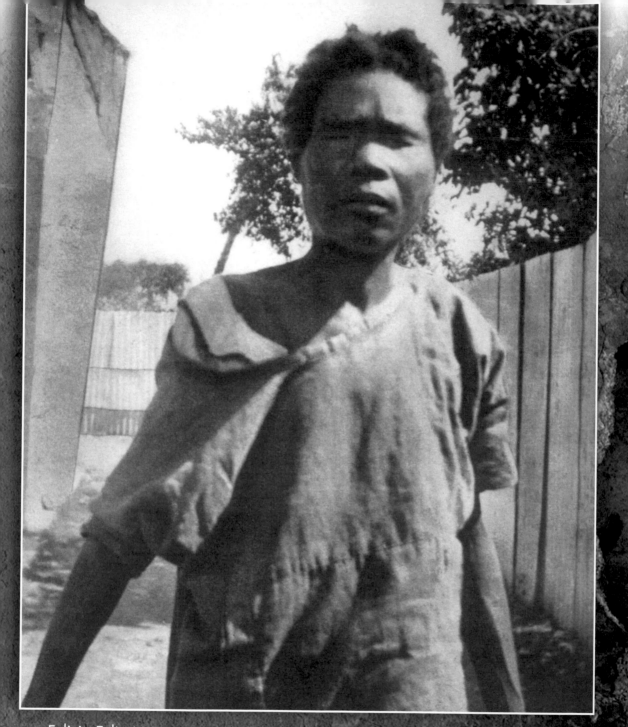

Felicia Felix-Mentor was a Haitian woman who died in 1907 and then reportedly returned from the dead—as a zombie—nearly thirty years later. Her case was widely studied by doctors and scholars.

The zombie that Hurston supposedly encountered was a woman named Felicia Felix-Mentor. Felix-Mentor had died suddenly in 1907, leaving behind her husband and young son. Nearly thirty years passed. Then one day, in 1936, a woman was found wandering along the road. She went to a farm and claimed she had once lived there. The owner of the farm recognized her as his sister. Her husband also identified her. They believed it was Felix-Mentor, even though she was supposed to have died. The woman was taken to a hospital, where Hurston observed her hiding in a corner. Hurston wrote, "The sight was dreadful. That blank face with the dead eyes…There was nothing that you could say to her or get from her except by looking at her, and the sight of this wreckage was too much to endure for long."

Ruling with Fear

In 1957, François Duvalier moved into power as Haiti's president. He was a cruel ruler, punishing and even killing people who spoke out against him. Duvalier's nickname was "Papa Doc," which came from his medical background. He claimed that he could heal people through voodoo rituals, but he also created fear by spreading stories that he drank blood and ate human flesh. He even encouraged the belief that he was a bokor who could make zombies that would be at his disposal. For his personal security guards, Duvalier relied on a band of brutal hit men called the Tonton Macoutes. They were named after a figure in Haitian folklore who captures and punishes misbehaving children. Some believed the Tonton Macoutes were actually zombies created by Duvalier.

François "Papa Doc" Duvalier was the president of Haiti from 1957 until his death in 1971. During his cruel dictatorship, he terrified people who believed he could create zombies.

A doctor in the case, Louis P. Mars, discounted much of Hurston's account. He said that a medical examination showed that the woman in question was probably not Felix-Mentor at all—dead or alive. As for her disturbing behavior, that was probably due to insanity, not zombiism.

Although Hurston did write of her belief in zombies, later in her account she also stated that she spoke with a doctor and concluded that zombies were not actually recalled from death. Instead, they had been drugged, causing them to lose their will and consciousness.

Clairvius Narcisse

"Angelina?"

Clairvius Narcisse approached his sister in a public market one day in 1980. She was surprised to see him, to say the least. Her brother did not visit often—because he had died eighteen years before!

Yet Angelina Narcisse was convinced that the man in front of her was her brother. Others who met him also vouched for his identity. There were things he knew that only the real Clairvius could have known. So how did this man, whom Angelina had seen buried back in 1962, still live?

Narcisse reported that he had been drugged and made into a zombie. He remembered being buried, and he remembered when the bokor came to get him from his coffin. He was then forced to work as a slave on a sugar plantation, which was difficult in his altered state. "The slightest chore required great effort," Narcisse reported later. His senses and perceptions were also damaged from the drugs. Narcisse said he literally could not see straight. To him, it seemed as though "my eyes were turned in."

After Narcisse had worked for two years, his bokor died. Narcisse was freed, but he did not return home. He was not on good terms with his brother, whom he suspected had turned him over to the bokor in the first place. He waited for years, until he heard his brother had died. Then he felt it was safe to go back. That was when he approached Angelina in the marketplace.

Narcisse's story caught the attention of an American professor named Wade Davis. Davis was an ethnobotanist, which is someone who studies how plants are used in various cultures. He wanted to see if there might be some scientific truth in what Narcisse had said. He went to Haiti and tested a sample of the poison that bokors used. He determined that one of its ingredients was tetrodotoxin, a powerful poison found in several animals, including puffer fish and certain toads. Tetrodotoxin can easily cause death. However, in low doses, it only paralyzes its victims temporarily—just long enough for a bokor to get to them. Then the people are revived only to be given another drug, found in a plant called the zombie cucumber, which keeps them in a dazed state.

Chapter 3

Throughout the South

The slave culture spread from Africa, through the Caribbean, and into the United States, where slaves were forced to work on huge plantations. They were excluded from white society, so they banded together with their own culture and belief systems. The low country of South Carolina, near Charleston, became another place where the voodoo religion took root.

For many believers, being zombified was the ultimate punishment. In many stories, the victim was someone who was not well liked. Revenge was a common reason why people were zombified. Other times, the victim was given as a sacrifice to a bokor in return for money or power. For slaves, zombies represented their life of servitude. But zombies' fates were even worse than those of slaves. For a zombie, not even death brought freedom.

The Black Constable

There was the law in Charleston, South Carolina, in the late 1800s, and then there was John Domingo. A constable is like a policeman, and people called John Domingo "the black constable" because he made his own laws—and they always suited him.

This 1920 etching shows black slaves working on a plantation. Slaves across the southern United States often practiced native religions such as voodoo.

Domingo did not worry about blending in. He wore an overcoat in all seasons and a silver ring shaped like a snake. He tied up his hair with shoelaces. People did not walk by his house if they could avoid it. Women would not brush their hair outside for fear that Domingo might get a lock of it and use it against them in a voodoo spell.

Domingo was known as a powerful voodoo king. According to legend, he cast harmful spells against those who angered him. He made one woman's laundry fall to pieces. He caused flowers that poisoned the bees to grow. He made it so that fires would not give any heat, only smoke.

Neighbors said they could hear the steps creaking at night at Domingo's house. They said it was from ghosts who had come to see him. And they said that he was a necromancer, someone who could raise the dead. People called him the "Zombi Man." They believed that he could create zombies whenever he wanted. Then he used them to run his graveyard errands, collecting supplies for his voodoo spells. Only God could stop him. John Bennett

Zombie Insects

Being a human zombie is bad enough. But what if you were not only stuck being a zombie, you also had to do it as a cockroach? If a cockroach is unfortunate enough to run into a jewel wasp, this might be its fate. First the female wasp stings the cockroach, paralyzing it. Then she lays her eggs in its abdomen so that her young will have a food source. Next she stings the cockroach's brain, injecting a poison that disables its escape reflex. She has created a zombie cockroach, which will now follow the wasp back to her burrow, where she can keep an eye on it.

Another species of wasp uses caterpillars as its victims. This wasp lays her eggs inside the caterpillar's body and injects it with a poison that turns off the caterpillar's immune system, ensuring that it will not kill the eggs.

wrote in *Doctor to the Dead*, "[Domingo] could call the dead back from the dust...that is, if no prayers had been spoken and no part of the service read. For then all he could do was of no avail. God Almighty would then have the departing spirit held firm in His hand."

Domingo brought one man back from the grave, but it was not a welcome homecoming. The man's family was not happy to see him. His heirs had already divided his property between them, and they did not want to give it back. Domingo sent him back to his grave. Another time, a man begged Domingo to raise his dead girlfriend. He did so, but the woman was not the same cheerful person she had been in life. She was only a zombie, and her boyfriend was relieved when Domingo released his hold on her and let her die again.

People knew not to mess with Domingo. They did not want to talk to him; they did not even want to talk about him. One neighbor said, "I could see what went on in that backyard." But he stopped there. "I would rather my neighbors not know that I talked about John Domingo."

Doctor Buzzard

In the 1920s, the most famous voodoo practitioner in the Charleston area was Doctor Buzzard. He was best known as a root worker. He used plants to make herbal remedies and other powders and potions.

Doctor Buzzard was also known as a courtroom specialist. During trials, strange visitors would sometimes appear in the courtroom and stare threateningly at witnesses. Afraid, these witnesses suddenly changed their testimony. People believed that these visitors had been sent by Doctor Buzzard. In fact, he had summoned them from the grave. Certainly, being stared down by a dead man would be a bit unnerving!

One man was not afraid to go up against Doctor Buzzard. Edward McTeer Jr. became the Beaufort County sheriff in 1926, after his father (the previous sheriff) died. McTeer suspected that Doctor Buzzard was causing the courtroom problems. He told Doctor Buzzard to stop, but it did not work. So McTeer stepped up his efforts. He decided to go after him. The fight waged

Voodoo practitioners like Doctor Buzzard used potions and herbal remedies to enchant victims. The artifacts shown here are replicas, not the actual objects used by Doctor Buzzard.

on, with neither man really winning. Finally, McTeer collected evidence to show Doctor Buzzard had been illegally giving out potions to use as medicine. He was able to arrest him for practicing medicine without a license. Facing legal trouble and fines, Doctor Buzzard got sick and then died. Or did he? People whispered that Doctor Buzzard was not really gone—he had turned himself into a cat to escape McTeer. Either way, the stories about him lived on.

Getting Philosophical

Imagine a human being that eats, sleeps, goes to school, and does all the other normal things people do. Now imagine that this person is doing all those things without really experiencing them. Philosophical zombies, or "p-zombies," are neither dead nor undead because they don't actually exist. P-zombies are a concept. They would be people who are biologically alive, but who lack the consciousness and senses that real people have. Philosophers and scientists who study how the mind works think the p-zombie is an interesting concept because it raises the question of what really makes someone human. How would these p-zombies come to be? One possibility is through science. With developing technology, doctors can implant chips in people's brains that can change their behavior. In addition, people could be electronically controlled by another person, or even a computer.

Xara, the Zombris

Just to the east of Louisiana, in Biloxi, Mississippi, a young woman was driving down the road one day in March of 2009. By the side of the road, she saw another woman walking. The woman had long, dark hair and was dressed in a loose white gown. The driver passed her, then glanced into her rearview mirror. What she saw was unnerving. The woman looked strange: her eyes had no pupils, and her skin was an unnatural shade of white. Then she faded away.

Intrigued—and perhaps frightened—by what she had seen, the driver began to ask people around town whether they had any knowledge of the mysterious woman. It turned out the town locals knew about her. They called her Xara, the Zombris. One man told her that Xara had been a Nicaraguan woman who was studying Santeria, a religion that is similar to voodoo.

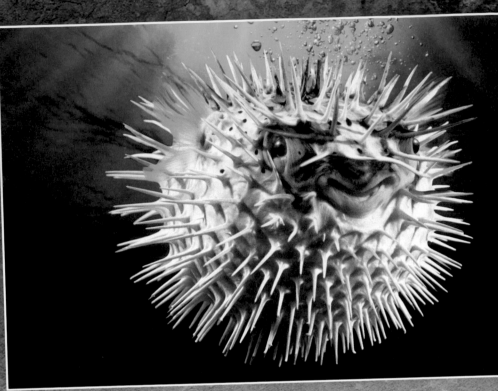

Although it's the spines that look scary, the bigger danger in the puffer fish is its powerful poison, used in zombie powder, which causes nerve damage and can kill people.

As part of her research, Xara traveled to New Orleans to learn from a voodoo priest. She became involved with this man, but he became angry when he found out she was disloyal. He used his power and poisoned her with the puffer fish toxin, turning her into a zombie. For a while, Xara remained completely under his control as she wandered the streets of New Orleans. Eventually, the priest released her and she returned to Mississippi.

Xara was a changed woman, simply walking around in a mindless trance. Then one day, a trucker picked her up on the road. No one ever saw her again. The story is that she was probably killed. As she wanders the streets now, she is caught in two supernatural traps, for she is both a ghost and a zombie.

Chapter 4

Zombies in Popular Culture

Zombies can't be beat. Sure, the heroes in movies might eventually win. They'll cut off the zombies' heads, or run them down with cars, or simply hole up in some remote fortress. Zombies aren't as mysterious as ghosts or as smart as vampires. But when it comes to pop culture power, zombies still rule.

The Evolution of Zombies

Zombies have changed over the years. They first came to the big screen with the 1932 movie *White Zombie*. The voodoo-created zombie in this movie played on people's distrust and fear of other cultures. Later, zombie movies tapped into a new fear: getting sick. In the 1950s and 1960s, zombies created from massive doses of radiation showed up. Not surprisingly, this was during the Cold War, when many Americans were worried about a nuclear attack. Other books and movies showed zombies as the result of widespread disease.

Hollywood gave zombies its own spin. Voodoo-created slaves might make for a good movie, but bloodied, undead monsters were even better. Although these zombies were mindless, they were not powerless, like voodoo zombies. They not only had the power to act, but they also wanted to kill living people. That made them even more frightening.

Bela Lugosi, Brandon Hurst, and Frederick Peters starred in the 1932 movie *White Zombie*, about a woman who is turned into a zombie while visiting Haiti.

However, zombies were not always audiences' monster of choice. Zombies only wanted to eat brains—they didn't have any themselves. "Hapless, not particularly scary or threatening…zombies were as low as you could go in the horror hierarchy," wrote David Flint in *Zombie Holocaust*. However, one thing zombies did have was strength in numbers. Maybe that was why they were able to push themselves out of the corny movies of the 1950s.

Zombies in Books, TV, and Movies

In 1968, director George Romero made a film called *Night of the Living Dead*. Although this was not the first zombie movie, it has since become a classic. People who study zombie movies (and there are a few!) say this film was a turning point. In this movie, zombies are not puppets whose strings are being pulled by some human master. Instead, they are acting for themselves. Unfortunately, their goal—eating living people—goes against all human instincts.

Zombies stagger across a field in *Night of the Living Dead*, a 1968 film in which a group of people take refuge in a farmhouse to hide from attacking zombies.

With this movie, Romero reinvented the zombie genre, and audiences, well, ate it up. The movie was a huge success. Romero followed it up with several sequels. Ten years later, in 1978, he released *Dawn of the Dead*. Next up was *Day of the Dead* in 1985. After that, Romero took a twenty-year break, but it turned out the Dead series wasn't dead. He released *Land of the Dead* in 2005, *Diary of the Dead* in 2007, and *Survival of the Dead* in 2009.

In *I Am Legend*, Will Smith plays a character who is one of the few survivors of a disease that has ravaged the world and turned people into brutal, zombie-like creatures.

By now, however, zombies were ready for a makeover. In 2002, the movie *28 Days Later* came out. Some say it helped breathe new life into the genre of zombie movies. Others argue that it's not really a zombie movie because there are no zombies. Instead, the villains of this movie are living, but they are infected with a horrible disease that makes them attack humans. However, aside from not being dead, they act very much

like zombies. They move in packs. They are relentless. And they have no human feelings to stop them.

In 1954, Richard Matheson wrote a book called *I Am Legend*. In it, a disease infects both the living and the dead, turning them into blood-thirsty killers. It seems that only one man has survived the infection. He spends his time trying to survive and defend himself in deserted Los Angeles. George Romero said that this book influenced him when he made *Night of the Living Dead*. Matheson's book was also used as the basis for several other movies, including *The Last Man on Earth* starring Vincent Price in 1964, and *I Am Legend* starring Will Smith in 2007. (For that movie, the setting was moved to New York City.) Another popular zombie book came out in 2006. Max Brooks's novel *World War Z* is a collection of stories telling how several people coped after a zombie disaster.

Recently, the television channel AMC aired a series called *The Walking Dead*. It follows a group of people who are trying to survive after most of the world has been taken over by zombies. Zombies have also made it into numerous comic books and video games, where players hunt and kill zombies — good practice if a real zombie apocalypse ever happens!

Walk, Don't Run

Their lunch is usually worse than whatever the school cafeteria is offering, but other than that, there are some advantages to being a zombie. No one is likely to pick a fight with you, for example. Since you're dead, you don't need to do homework and chores. And you never have to worry about whether you look good. (You don't.)

Actually, being a zombie can be kind of fun. That's probably why "zombie walks" are becoming popular in cities across the United States. The first zombie walk was held in 2001, in San Francisco, California, as a way to promote a film festival. Since then, they have been held as mock political rallies and as ways to raise money for charities. And some of them are just for fun.

Participants dress up as zombies and shamble through the streets. Sometimes they even capture and "zombify" a few victims. They will pull them from the crowd and pretend to attack them. What they are really doing, however, is giving these people a quick makeover: dressing them in ragged clothing and applying some zombie makeup to make it look like they have been converted into zombies themselves.

In Pittsburgh, Pennsylvania—where George Romero attended film school—an annual Zombie Fest is held. The event features brain-eating contests and a competition to see who is the ugliest. The city holds the record for the largest zombie walk ever. In 2010, more than 4,500 people participated.

Zombies walk the streets in 2010 in Mexico City, Mexico. Zombie walks have become popular in cities around the world and are often organized to raise money for charity.

Surviving the Zombie Apocalypse

In reality, dead people do not come back as brain-munching monsters. Living people infected by viruses either get better or die and stay dead. But that's the real world. The scary scenario of a zombie-infested world may be fiction, but it's also fun. Zombies have taken over the imaginations of authors, filmmakers, and audiences. They have turned the idea of the zombie apocalypse into its own game.

In 2003, author Max Brooks published *The Zombie Survival Guide*. This is a humor book, but it takes a pretend serious approach. It tells people how to protect themselves from zombies and how to fight them if necessary. There are chapters explaining what weapons to use (avoid guns: the noise might attract more zombies); how to protect yourself in different structures (go upstairs, then destroy the staircase); and what kinds of transportation work best (bicycles don't require gas, but be sure to wear a helmet).

Warning! Zombies Ahead!

Drivers on a highway near Tucson, Arizona, got a surprise one day in November 2010. The message on a portable street sign read "Zombies Ahead." Mischievous hackers had managed to break into the electronic system and change the sign's message. (Unfortunately, it did not provide directions for a detour.) Police called the incident a prank. "We didn't get any…reports of zombies," one said. The same thing happened in January 2009, in Texas. There, a spokesman for the state's Department of Transportation admitted, "It was clever, kind of cute, but not at all what [the sign] was intended for." Tampering with street signs is illegal, too. If the people who did it got caught, they could get fined or even go to jail—if the zombies did not get them first.

There are also Web sites that pretend to show people how to survive in a world that's been zombified. Some of these are just plain fun, but others combine real-world survival techniques with the interest factor of zombies. The Zombie Squad, for example, advertises that it will provide "zombie removal" services to those who have an infestation. In reality, the Zombie Squad provides classes on how to prepare for more likely disasters, such as earthquakes or floods. In addition, the Zombie Squad holds zombie-themed charity events to raise money for organizations such as the American Red Cross.

The popularity of zombies is easy to see in books and movies, on the Internet, and on the streets of cities across the United States. In some ways, they've already taken over. These zombies would not exist without the brains of authors and filmmakers, but fortunately, it's not because they ate them!

Glossary

antebellum Dating to before the American Civil War.

apocalypse A disaster that results in a world completely changed for the worse.

bokor A voodoo practitioner who can create zombies.

casualty An injury or death caused by war.

genre A category or type.

gris-gris A small bag of charmed items that is worn as protection.

hapless Ineffective or useless.

heir A person who inherits money or property from someone who dies.

hierarchy The order of importance.

infested Inhabited with a large number; overrun.

lethargic Very tired; lacking energy.

mock Pretend.

necromancer Someone who summons the spirits of dead people or brings them back to life.

paraphernalia Equipment and supplies related to a certain practice.

reanimated Having been given the appearance of life.

resurrected Brought back from death.

scoff To scorn; show disbelief in a rude manner.

sequel A follow-up to a story.

shamble To shuffle; walk slowly.

superstition A belief that does not have a basis in reason but is often widely accepted.

underling Someone with less power or status.

vouch To confirm; express belief in something.

For More Information

American Museum of Natural History
Central Park West at 79th Street
New York, NY 10024-5192
(212) 769-5100
Web site: http://www.amnh.org
The museum features exhibits covering a wide array of human history
    and culture relating to the natural world. An online exhibit about
    Haiti and the traditions that helped give rise to the idea of
    zombiism can be viewed at the museum's Web site, at http://
    www.amnh.org/exhibitions/vodou.

Haitian Heritage Museum
4141 NE 2 Avenue, #105C
Miami, FL 33137
(305) 371-5988
Web site: http://www.haitianheritagemuseum.org
Through exhibits and educational outreach programs, the museum seeks
    to preserve the history and heritage of the Haitian people.

Monroeville Zombies
161 Monroeville Mall
Monroeville, PA 15146
(412) 373-4303
Web site: http://www.monroevillezombies.com
Located in the mall where *Dawn of the Dead* was filmed in 1978,
    this museum offers exhibits celebrating zombies in popular
    culture.

New Orleans Voodoo Museum
724 Dumaine Street
New Orleans, LA 70116
(504) 680-0128
Web site: http://www.voodoomuseum.com
Through a variety of exhibits, this independent museum works to preserve the
  history of New Orleans's voodoo culture.

Oyotunji African Village
P.O. Box 51
Sheldon, SC 29941
(843) 846-8900
Web site: http://www.oyotunjiafricanvillage.org
Founded in the 1970s, this authentic African village in South Carolina is
  devoted to preserving African traditions, including the Yoruba religion
  from which voodoo comes.

Rue Morgue
2926 Dundas Street West
Toronto, ON M6P 1Y8
Canada
(416) 651-9675
Web site: http://www.rue-morgue.com
Founded in 1997, this Canadian magazine is dedicated to reporting on the
  horror genre in film, television, and other media.

ZombieMall.com
c/o Brian Hardin II
35 Lusk Street
Batesville, AR 72501
Web site: http://www.zombiemall.com
ZombieMall offers zombie-themed merchandise for sale, as well as a blog featur-
  ing interviews, reviews, and commentary about zombie popular culture.

Zombie Squad, Inc.
P.O. Box 63124
St. Louis, MO 63163-3124
(888) 495-4052
Web site: http://www.zombiehunters.org
The Zombie Squad purports to be a company for exterminating zombies;
    however, when business is "slow," it focuses on teaching general sur-
    vival techniques.

Web Sites

Due to the changing nature of Internet links, Rosen Publishing has developed
an online list of Web sites related to the subject of this book. This site is
updated regularly. Please use this link to access the list:

http://www.rosenlinks.com/amss/zomb

For Further Reading

Ashby, Amanda. *Zombie Queen of Newbury High*. New York, NY: Speak, 2009.

Dendle, Peter. *The Zombie Movie Encyclopedia*. Jefferson, NC: McFarland, 2010.

Forget, Thomas. *Introducing Zombies* (Famous Movie Monsters). New York, NY: Rosen Publishing, 2006.

Ganeri, Anita. *Vampires and the Undead* (The Dark Side). New York, NY: PowerKids Press, 2010.

Gee, Joshua. *Encyclopedia Horrifica: The Terrifying TRUTH! About Vampires, Ghosts, Monsters, and More*. New York, NY: Scholastic, 2007.

Gritzner, Charles. *Haiti* (Modern World Nations). New York, NY: Chelsea House Publications, 2011.

Guiley, Rosemary Ellen, and Jeanne Keyes Youngson. *The Encyclopedia of Vampires, Werewolves, and Other Monsters*. New York, NY: Checkmark Books, 2004.

Hamilton, Sue. *Zombies*. Edina, MN: ABDO Publishing, 2007.

Jenson-Elliott, Cynthia. *Zombies*. Farmington Hills, MI: Kidhaven Press, 2007.

Kloepfer, John. *The Zombie Chasers*. New York, NY: Harper, 2010.

Krensky, Stephen. *Zombies*. Minneapolis, MN: Lerner Publications, 2008.

Lyons, Mary E. *Sorrow's Kitchen: The Life and Folklore of Zora Neale Hurston*. New York, NY: Atheneum, 1993.

Person, Stephen. *Voodoo in New Orleans* (Horrorscapes). New York, NY: Bearport Publishing, 2010.

Pipe, Jim. *Zombies* (Tales of Horror). New York, NY: Bearport Publishing, 2006.

Schuh, Mari, and Aaron Sautter. *Zombies* (Blazers). Mankato, MN: Capstone Press, 2006.

Shone, Rob. *Zombies: Tales of the Living Dead*. New York, NY: Rosen Publishing, 2011.

Sleator, William. *The Boy Who Couldn't Die*. New York, NY: Harry N. Abrams, Inc., 2004.

Stefoff, Rebecca. *Vampires, Zombies, and Shape-Shifters*. Tarrytown, NY: Marshall Cavendish Benchmark, 2008.

Valentino, Serena. *How to Be a Zombie: The Essential Guide for Anyone Who Craves Brains*. Somerville, MA: Candlewick Press, 2010.

Van Lowe, E. *Never Slow Dance with a Zombie*. New York, NY: Tor Books, 2009.

Bibliography

Ackermann, Hans W., and Jeanine Gauthier. "The Ways and Nature of the Zombi." *Journal of American Folklore*, Vol. 104, No. 414, 1991, pp. 466–494.

Bennett, John. *The Doctor to the Dead: Grotesque Legends and Folk Tales of Old Charleston*. New York, NY: Rinehart & Company, 1946.

Bishop, Kyle William. *American Zombie Gothic: The Rise and Fall (and Rise) of the Walking Dead in Popular Culture*. Jefferson, NC: McFarland and Company, 2010.

Brooks, Max. *The Zombie Survival Guide: Complete Protection from the Living Dead*. New York, NY: Three Rivers Press, 2003.

Brown, Nathan Robert. *The Complete Idiot's Guide to Zombies*. New York, NY: Penguin, 2010.

Curran, Bob. *Encyclopedia of the Undead: A Field Guide to Creatures That Cannot Rest in Peace*. Franklin Lakes, NJ: New Page Books, 2006.

Davis, Wade. *The Serpent and the Rainbow*. New York, NY: Simon and Schuster, 1997.

Dayan, Joan. *Haiti, History, and the Gods*. Berkeley, CA: University of California Press, 1995.

Diederich, Bernard, and Claudia Wallis. "Medicine: Zombies: Do They Exist?" *Time*, October 17, 1983. Retrieved February 2, 2011 (http://www.time.com/time/magazine/article/0,9171,952208-1,00.html).

Farson, Daniel. *Vampires, Zombies, and Monster Men*. New York, NY: Doubleday and Company, 1976.

Flint, David. *Zombie Holocaust: How the Living Dead Devoured Pop Culture*. London, England: Plexus Publishing, 2009.

Hurston, Zora Neale. *Tell My Horse: Voodoo and Life in Haiti and Jamaica*. New York, NY: Harper and Row, 1990.

Maberry, Jonathan. *Zombie CSU: The Forensics of the Living Dead*. New York, NY: Citadel Press Books, 2008.

Mars, Louis P. "The Story of Zombi in Haiti." *Man: A Record of Anthropological Science*, Vol. XLV, No. 22, March–April 1945, pp. 38–40.

McIntosh, Shawn, and Marc Leverette. *Zombie Culture: Autopsies of the Living Dead*. Lanham, MD: Scarecrow Press, 2008.

Métraux, Alfred, translated by Hugo Charteris. *Voodoo in Haiti*. New York, NY: Shocken Books, 1972.

Monstrous.com. "Voodoo Zombies." Retrieved February 2, 2011 (http://zombies.monstrous.com/voodoo_zombies.htm).

Roberts, Paul Dale. "Xara the Zombris." Unexplained-mysteries.com, September 15, 2009. Retrieved February 4, 2011 (http://www.unexplained-mysteries.com/column.php?id=163995).

Seabrook, William B. *The Magic Island*. New York, NY: Harcourt, Brace and Company, 1929.

Steiger, Brad. *Real Zombies, The Living Dead, and Creatures of the Apocalypse*. Canton, MI: Visible Ink Press, 2010.

Tallant, Robert. *Voodoo in New Orleans*. New York, NY: The Macmillan Company, 1946.

Index

About the Author

Diane Bailey has written more than twenty books for children and young adults, including ones on the supernatural creatures, ghosts, and vampires. She has two sons and lives in Kansas, where she writes, edits, and stays out of graveyards at night.

Photo Credits

Cover, p. 1 Dieter Spears/Vetta/Getty Images; cover, back cover, interior background image © www.istockphoto.com/Dusko Jovic; pp. 3, 6, 14, 22, 29 (silhouette) © www.istockphoto.com/Kevin Cochran; p. 4 Kris Conner/Getty Images; p. 7 Purestock/Getty Images; p. 8 © Jeff Greenberg/The Image Works; p. 10 Photos.com/Thinkstock; pp. 12, 17 © Mary Evans Picture Library/The Image Works; p. 15 Romano Cagnoni/Hulton Archive/Getty Images; p. 19 Robert Lerner/Hulton Archive/Getty Images; p. 23 Time & Life Pictures/Getty Images; p. 26 Shutterstock.com; p. 28 Steven Hunt/Stone/Getty Images; p. 30 Courtesy Everett Collection; p. 31 Photo by New Line Cinemas/Zuma Press © Copyright 2006 New Line Cinemas; pp. 32–33 © Overbrook Entertainment/Entertainment Pictures/Zuma Press; pp. 34–35 Alfredo Estrella/AFP/Getty Images.

Designer: Nicole Russo; Editor: Bethany Bryan; Photo Researcher: Karen Huang